WOMEN IN SCIENCE
ADA LOVELACE

Written by
Nick Pierce

Illustrated by
Isobel Lundie

Franklin Watts®
An Imprint of Scholastic Inc.

Author:

Nick Pierce graduated from the University of Oxford with a degree in English. He has worked in television production and publishing. He is also a writer, specializing in history and information titles for children.

Artist:

Isobel Lundie graduated from Kingston University in 2015 where she studied illustration and animation. She is interested in how colorful and distinctive artwork can transform stories for children.

Photo credits:
p.15 Industrialisation: 19th c. town in Lancashire. Credit: Wellcome Collection. CC BY Shutterstock and Wikimedia Commons.

PAPER FROM SUSTAINABLE FORESTS

Published in Great Britain in 2020 by
The Salariya Book Company Ltd
25 Marlborough Place, Brighton BN1 1UB

Library of Congress Cataloging-in-Publication Data

Names: Pierce, Nick, author. | Lundie, Isobel, illustrator.
Title: Ada Lovelace / Nick Pierce ; illustrator, Isobel Lundie.
Description: New York : Franklin Watts®, an imprint of Scholastic Inc., 2020.
 | Series: Women in science | "Published in Great Britain in 2019 by Book
 House, an imprint of The Salariya Book Company Ltd." | Includes index.
Identifiers: LCCN 2019008972| ISBN 9780531235348 (library binding) | ISBN
 9780531239513 (pbk.)
Subjects: LCSH: Lovelace, Ada King, Countess of, 1815-1852--Juvenile
 literature. | Women mathematicians--Great Britain--Biography--Juvenile
 literature. | Mathematicians--Great Britain--Biography--Juvenile
 literature. | Computers--History--19th century -Juvenile literature.
Classification: LCC QA29.L72 P54 2020 | DDC 510.92 [B] --dc23

Printed and bound in China.
Printed on paper from sustainable sources.
1 2 3 4 5 6 7 8 9 10 R 27 26 25 24 23 22 21 20

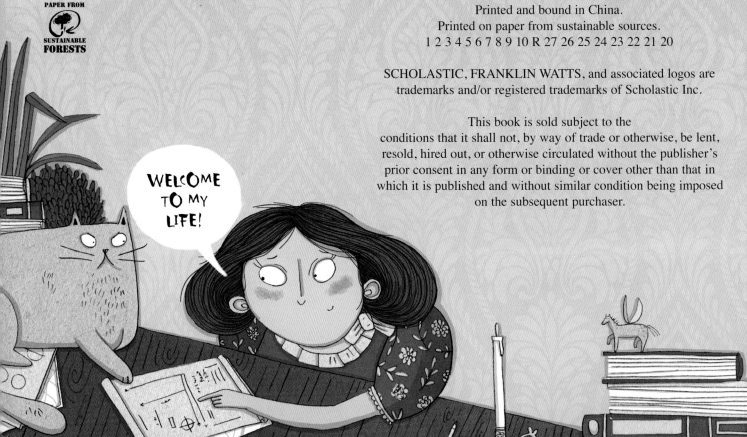

CONTENTS PAGE

ADA LOVELACE

ImPORTANT PLACES IN ADA'S LIFE

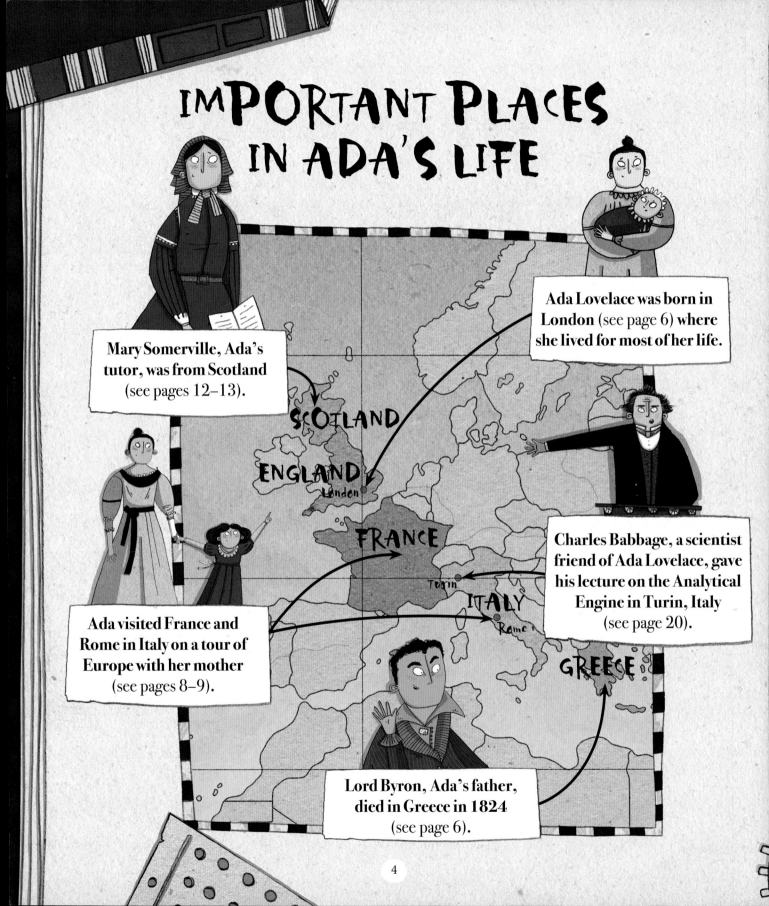

Mary Somerville, Ada's tutor, was from Scotland (see pages 12–13).

Ada Lovelace was born in London (see page 6) where she lived for most of her life.

Ada visited France and Rome in Italy on a tour of Europe with her mother (see pages 8–9).

Charles Babbage, a scientist friend of Ada Lovelace, gave his lecture on the Analytical Engine in Turin, Italy (see page 20).

Lord Byron, Ada's father, died in Greece in 1824 (see page 6).

SCOTLAND

ENGLAND

London

FRANCE

Turin

ITALY

Rome

GREECE

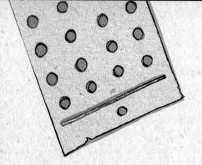

INTRODUCTION

Throughout history, there have always been women scientists. But because they often didn't have the right to work in professional jobs, their work—often alongside fathers, husbands, or brothers—was generally ignored. Over recent decades, historians have uncovered the little-known achievements of many women scientists and now they are starting to get the attention they deserve.

Ada Lovelace's brilliant talent for mathematics and huge imagination helped to pave the way for the invention of the computer **software** that powers the world around us. Every time you play a computer game or talk with a friend on your smartphone, you can only do so because of the **pioneering** work by Ada Lovelace.

Her work was groundbreaking. Unlike her poet father, Lord Byron, she was not a famous figure during her lifetime. However, she became known to those who knew her as the "enchantress of number." This book tells Ada's story.

ADA'S CHILDHOOD

Augusta Ada Byron was born in 1815. She was the daughter of Anne Isabella Milbanke, a highly educated woman, and Lord Byron, a famous Romantic poet. Ada never really knew her father, as he left the family home to live in mainland Europe when she was just a baby.

I'M A GENIUS!

POEMS LORD BYRON

Lord Byron

George Gordon Byron wrote poems that made him famous in nineteenth century Europe. He was also well known for restlessly traveling around Europe. His friends described him as "mad, bad, and dangerous to know." He died of a fever in Missolonghi, Greece while trying to help the Greeks achieve independence from Turkish rule, aged thirty-six. His poetry lives on to this day.

Hard Study

When she was very young, Ada moved with her mother into Anne's parents' home, where she would be given a strict upbringing. Anne, who had a great interest in science and mathematics, made her daughter study these subjects hard. Fortunately, Ada also had her beloved pet cat for company, Mrs. Puff, alongside the endless math problems!

YOU FORGOT TO CARRY THE ONE.

Mrs. Puff

I'M FREE AS A BIRD!

Imagination

Ada's imagination could never be controlled—she was always coming up with strange and exciting ideas. We'll look at some of them more closely later in the book.

Ada as a child

A TRIP AROUND EUROPE

When Ada was ten, her mother took her on a tour around Europe. The trip allowed Ada to improve her French and to see some of the scientific developments taking place on the continent.

The Pantheon

EUROPE IS BEAUTIFUL.

The Math of Buildings

On the trip, Ada learned that the designers of buildings like the **Pantheon** in Rome, with its enormous dome, used mathematical knowledge in all their work. This led her to see the amazing ways that math can be used to transform the world around us.

FIG 1. ASTRONOMY

FIG 2. BIOLOGY

FIG 3. CHEMISTRY

Language of Numbers

She also started to see links between the language she was learning and numbers. She came to see numbers as a language themselves that could be put into different patterns.

An Explosion of Science

In the late 1700s and early 1800s science became very important. There were big breakthroughs in **biology**, **chemistry**, **astronomy**, and **physics**. Ada would meet and learn from many of the scientists leading this **revolution**.

WHAT DO YOU THINK, MRS. PUFF?

ADA'S FLYING MACHINE

While visiting parks and watching birds flying overhead, Ada had the idea to build a flying **machine** for humans. In 1828, this would become her first scientific project. Ada took the project very seriously.

" ...a thing in the form of a horse with a steam engine in the inside so contrived as to move an immense pair of wings, fixed on the outside of the horse... " —Ada Lovelace

I HATE ALL THIS HORSING AROUND.

Ada's Research

She wrote down her observations on the length and width of birds' wings and how they move them to swoop through the air. She also thought about which materials would be best for building a human flying machine.

Leonardo Da Vinci

Scientists and artists have been fascinated by flight for centuries. The Italian artist and engineer Leonardo da Vinci made detailed drawings of machines that could fly.

WHAT A RIDE!

FLYOLOGY
ADA LOVELACE

Ada put down her thoughts in a book she called *Flyology*. The project was an early training ground for her scientific and imaginative ways of thinking.

FLYOLOGY
ADA LOVELACE

A BRILLIANT TUTOR

At this time, Ada came down with a serious case of measles—a very deadly disease in the nineteenth century. Ada was kept in bed for over a year while she recovered from the illness. She then had to use crutches for a while to walk around. Ada's luck improved when she met her new tutor, Mary Somerville.

Mary Somerville, (1780–1872)

Mary Somerville

Mary Somerville was a brilliant Scottish scientist. Her scientific work covered chemistry, physics, mathematics, **geology**, and astronomy, and earned her glowing reviews from the other leading scientific minds of her day.

A Pioneering Astronomer

Mary Somerville carried out experiments to better understand the qualities of light and magnetism, and she loved to study the stars and the solar system. She predicted the existence of an undiscovered planet that was affecting the gravity of Uranus. Her work in this field helped to lead to the discovery of Neptune in 1846.

URANUS

HMMM, I WONDER...

YOU'RE IMPROVING ALL THE TIME, ADA.

Progress

With the support and encouragement of Mary Somerville and her mother, Ada made real progress in several sciences and took on more and more advanced work in mathematics.

A bestseller

Mary Somerville's *On The Connexion of the Physical Sciences*, published in 1834, was one of the bestselling science books of the nineteenth century.

THE DAILY POST
MARY SOMERVILLE'S OBITUARY IN 1872:

Whatever difficulty we might experience in the middle of the nineteenth century in choosing a king of science, there could be no question whatever as to the queen of science.

13

THE JACQUARD LOOM

Ada and her mother visited local factories to see the amazing new machines that were transforming the way things were made. This transformation is now known as the Industrial Revolution. One day they saw the **Jacquard Loom**. **Looms** were machines that allowed an operator to weave complicated patterns from yarn or thread. The Jacquard Loom was different—and revolutionary—because it didn't need an operator to reset the bits of the loom for each new row of a **woven** design. It did this automatically.

AMAZING!

Punch cards

The Jacquard Loom used a series of cards with holes punched in each one. The pattern of holes on a card would be "read" by the loom, which would weave a row according to those instructions. Many cards could be strung together and fed into the loom so that rows of woven material would be produced. It was much faster than having a person change the settings for each row.

I HAVE AN IDEA.

Talking To Machines

Ada understood that the patterns of holes on the cards were a kind of language. She realized that this number language could be used to "talk" to machines, like the Jacquard Loom, and have them carry out operations on their own. This was the moment of inspiration that led to her developing the idea for computer programming.

HOW WOULD IT WORK?

THE DAILY NEWS

THE INDUSTRIAL REVOLUTION

The Industrial Revolution in Britain and in other countries was driven by steam power. Before steam power, people needed to use cattle, horses, or the force of running water to move machinery.

15

ADA'S NEW BEST FRIEND

At the same time, Ada began to hear about Charles Babbage's idea for the **Difference Engine**: A machine that could work out **calculations** mechanically when an operator gave it instructions.

Small prototype of the Difference Engine

MR. BABBAGE?

MISS BYRON?

Meeting Babbage

On June 5, 1833, Ada was introduced to Babbage by Mary Somerville at a party in London. Babbage invited Ada to see a completed model of the Difference Engine. It could work out mathematical problems mechanically. It had metal **gears** and rods, with numbered dials to provide the answers.

Sharing Ideas

Ada and Babbage found that they shared a lot of the same ideas and interests. They were both fascinated by the links between math and language, and the ways in which the "coding" of punched cards could play a part in allowing a machine to perform calculations. Babbage had also begun to imagine a machine more advanced even than the Difference Engine he had started to build—he called it the **Analytical Engine**.

BEHOLD: THE DIFFERENCE ENGINE!

Charles Babbage

Charles Babbage was a very important figure in nineteenth century British science. He had studied and taught at Cambridge University, where he held the post of Lucasian Professor of Mathematics—a position that had been previously held by Isaac Newton. He also helped to establish the Astronomical Society in 1820. But he is most famous for using his mathematical skill to also help develop the first modern computers.

BECOMING ADA LOVELACE

In 1835, when she was still only nineteen, Ada met and married Lord William King-Noel, a wealthy and older aristocrat. When Lord William's father died in 1838, he inherited the title of the First **Earl** of Lovelace, and Ada became the **Countess** of Lovelace. She had three children with Lord William and continued her studies in science and mathematics.

Augustus De Morgan

Lord William King-Noel

Professor De Morgan

Ada studied the plans for the Difference Engine given to her by Charles Babbage, until she understood the machine as well as its creator. From 1840–1841, she exchanged letters and calculations with Professor Augustus De Morgan of University College London as he taught her the highest levels of mathematics. This education gave Ada the technical knowledge she would need to make her scientific breakthrough.

$B_0 = 1$ $B_1 = \frac{-1}{2}$ $B_2 = \frac{1}{6}$ $B_4 =$

$S(11,4) = 39974$

$S(m,n) = \sum\limits_{k=1}^{B} k^n$

$Poly(m,n) =$

$Poly(11,4) =$

$\frac{1}{n+1} B_0 m^{n+1}$

$B_1 m^n + \frac{n}{2} =$

$\frac{n(n+1)(n-2)}{4}$

$\sum\limits_{k=1}^{m} k^n = 4.07$

$\frac{m^{n+1}(n+1)(n-)}{k^n}$

$K = B_1 m^2 + \frac{n}{2}(3$

$Poly(11,4) m^n$

THE TIMES
EXPLORATION AND DISCOVERY

OTHER NOTABLE SCIENTISTS OF THE NINETEENTH CENTURY

The early nineteenth century, when Ada was expanding her knowledge, was a period of great achievements in exploration and discovery. In the 1830s, at the same time that Ada Lovelace was studying the Difference Engine, a lot else was happening. Charles Darwin voyaged on the HMS Beagle and began to develop his theory of evolution by natural selection. Michael Faraday did experiments with electricity and magnetism and the links between the two.

CHARLES DARWIN

MICHAEL FARADAY

HMS BEAGLE

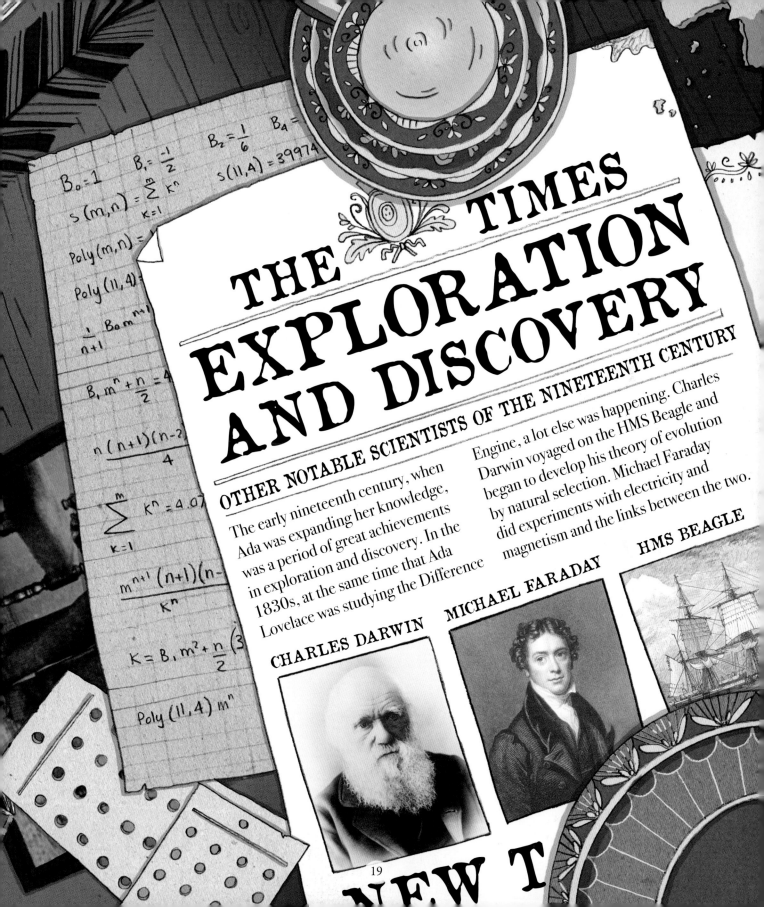

NEW T

In 1840, Babbage agreed to give a talk in Turin in northern Italy about his idea for the Analytical Engine. The Analytical Engine would read cards with holes punched in them, like the Jacquard loom. These cards would contain a language of numbers that would allow the engine to perform much more complex calculations than the Difference Engine, similar to a modern computer.

AN EXTREMELY IMPORTANT TALK

A Success

The talk was a success: many of the scientists in the audience saw the potential of Babbage's new machine. One of the audience members, Federico Luigi Menabrea, wrote up Babbage's thoughts and published them in French in a Swiss journal. This became the first published account of Babbage's invention.

INGENIOUS!

GOSH!

HOORAY!

SPLENDID!

The Analytical Engine

The Analytical Engine marked real progress in technology. It was really much more like the beginnings of a real computer than the Difference Engine. It could do many mathematical jobs and could store information (like a modern computer's memory) while it worked out other tasks.

The Difference Engine

De Morgan

HMPH! WHAT A WASTE OF MY TIME.

BRAVO!

Meanwhile...

Ada was stuck at home. She was worried that she wouldn't be taken seriously as a **mathematician**, because even her teacher De Morgan had a skeptical opinion of women's abilities. But math and science were Ada's passions and she kept on studying very hard. She was determined to prove herself and show the world.

AN UNUSUAL TRANSLATION

Ada decided that she was the best person to translate Menabrea's account into English because she was one of the few people who could speak French and understood the meaning of the words about the Analytical Engine.

A model of the Analytical Engine

An A to G of Notes

Ada showed her translation of the account to Babbage, who encouraged her to add her own thoughts at the end. Ada seized the opportunity, writing a series of notes, one for each letter of the alphabet from A to G, on the Analytical Engine and its potential. These notes showed the power of her imagination when applied to science.

I HAVE SO MUCH TO SAY. HOW SHOULD I PUT IT?

22

Machine Music?

Ada had long believed that music had a close relationship with mathematics. Both are logical and allow themselves to be expressed in a certain language. So if the Analytical Engine could work out advanced calculations on its own using numbers, then perhaps it could do something of the same with music? Perhaps such an engine could go so far as to compose music?

Published

The work was published, without Ada's name attached to it, as "Sketch of the Analytical Engine Invented by Charles Babbage...with Notes from the Translator." It appeared in 1843 as part of a highly respected series of scientific papers. This work would allow future scientists to build on Ada's and Babbage's ideas to invent computer technology.

THIS WILL CHANGE THE WORLD!

Charles Babbage

ENCHANTRESS OF NUMBER

Even though Ada was not linked with the work publicly until 1848, Babbage was very grateful to her for her ideas and contributions. He called her "the enchantress of number" because of her great mathematical ability and vision.

Poor Health

Sadly, Ada's health got worse and prevented her from doing more mathematical work at the same level as that shown in the "Sketch of the Analytical Engine..." After suffering from the effects of **cancer** for many years, she finally died, at age thirty-six, at home on November 27, 1852.

Ada and Mesmerism

One of Ada Lovelace's interests in her last years was a "scientific" process called Mesmerism.

Mesmerism was named after a German doctor, Franz Mesmer, who believed that living things were filled with an invisible force—like magnetism—that could be controlled. He claimed that sick people could be healed using this magnetic force, but the scientific world rejected his claims. However, Mesmer's work helped develop the more widely accepted practice of hypnosis.

ADA'S LEGACY

In the "Sketch of the Analytical Engine" Ada had introduced the idea of **algorithms**, which would allow the software that runs the computers of the twenty-first century to be developed. Algorithms are step-by-step commands that lead to the solution of a problem. Modern computers depend on a series of algorithms contained in their software to perform tasks, from the simplest sums to the most complicated calculations.

ADA IS WATCHING OVER US.

SMILE!

Punch cards

Ada's use of punched cards (inspired by the Jacquard Loom) was an example of algorithms at work. And when she proposed using the system to work out series of extremely complicated numbers, in the notes of her translation, she really produced the first computer program.

Instructions

She showed that, by using a code, or language, embedded in the punched cards, a person could instruct the engine to perform a task and then go on to perform another, and another, and another.

Computer Brain

Each stage in this progression could become more advanced, more closely acting in the way our own human brains think.

THE TELEGRAPH
LOVELACE DAY!

Ada Lovelace Day

Recognition of Ada's achievements is now widespread. The computer language used by the United States Department of Defense is called "Ada." Since 2009, an Ada Lovelace Day is held on the second Tuesday of October to celebrate every woman scientist and mathematician. And each year, on Ada Lovelace Day, the "Google Doodle" displays images relating to Ada and her work.

Girls using computers

TIMELINE OF ADA'S LIFE

1826-1828
Ada and her mother travel on a grand tour of Europe.

1816
Ada's parents, Lord and Lady Byron, separate, and Lord Byron moves to the European continent.

1833
Ada is introduced to Charles Babbage by Mary Somerville.

1822
Charles Babbage invents the Difference Engine.

1815
Augusta Ada Byron (Ada Lovelace) is born in London on December 10.

1828
Ada designs a flying machine after observing the flight of birds.

1835
Ada marries William King-Noel.

1824
Lord Byron dies in Greece during the Greek War of Independence.

1840
Charles Babbage's lecture on the Analytical Engine is delivered in Turin.

1936
Mathematician Alan Turing builds on the ideas of Lovelace and Babbage, proposing the concept of a universal machine, or Turing machine, that can compute anything that is computable. This concept will become the modern computer.

1842
Menabrea's French-language copy of Babbage's lecture is published in Geneva, Switzerland.

1959
The first computer language, COBOL, is introduced. It is based on work by the computer scientist, Grace Hopper.

1838
Ada becomes Countess of Lovelace after her husband becomes the Earl of Lovelace.

1974
Personal computers that can be used at home by ordinary people start to be sold on the market.

1842–1843
Ada Lovelace translates the French version of Babbage's lecture into English and adds her own notes at the end.

1852
Ada Lovelace dies on November 27.

GLOSSARY

Algorithm
A step-by-step method of solving a problem; computers rely on algorithms to perform complicated calculations.

Analytical Engine
The name that Charles Babbage gave to his planned calculating and computing machine that was more advanced than the earlier Difference Engine.

Astronomy
The scientific study of things beyond our own planet, such as the Moon, planets, and other stars.

Biology
The scientific study of living things, such as animals, plants, and humans.

Calculations
Answers to problems found using the basic operations of math: addition, subtraction, multiplication, and division.

Cancer
A growth in the human body that is often hard to control and which can lead to death.

Chemistry
The scientific study of the different substances from which everything in the universe is made, including their properties and how they interact.

Countess
A female aristocratic title given to the wife or widow of a British earl.

Difference Engine
The first of Charles Babbage's two calculating machines, the Difference Engine was designed to work out difficult problems using addition and subtraction. Babbage abandoned plans to build the Difference Engine because he turned his attention to the more advanced Analytical Engine.

Earl
One of the highest aristocratic titles that are ranked just below the level of king or queen.